GREAT
BUILDING
FEATS

THE CHANNEL TUNNEL

SANDY DONOVAN

Lerner Publications Company
Minneapolis

For Henry

Lerner Publications Company
A division of Lerner Publishing Group
241 First Avenue North
Minneapolis, MN 55401 U.S.A.

Website address: www.lernerbooks.com

Library of Congress Cataloging-in-Publication Data

Donovan, Sandra, 1967–
    The Channel Tunnel / by Sandra Donovan.
      p.   cm. — (Great building feats)
    Includes bibliographical references and index.
    Summary: A history of the building of the Channel Tunnel, which connects England and France, with emphasis on the difficulties of digging a tunnel where some engineers said it could not be done.
    ISBN: 0–8225–4692–2 (lib. bdg. : alk. paper)
    1. Channel Tunnel (England and France)—Juvenile literature. [1. Channel Tunnel (England and France) 2. Railroad tunnels—English Channel. 3. Tunnels] I. Title. II. Series.
TF238.C4D66 2003
624.1'94'0916336—dc21   2002012554

Manufactured in the United States of America
1 2 3 4 5 6 – JR – 08 07 06 05 04 03

CONTENTS

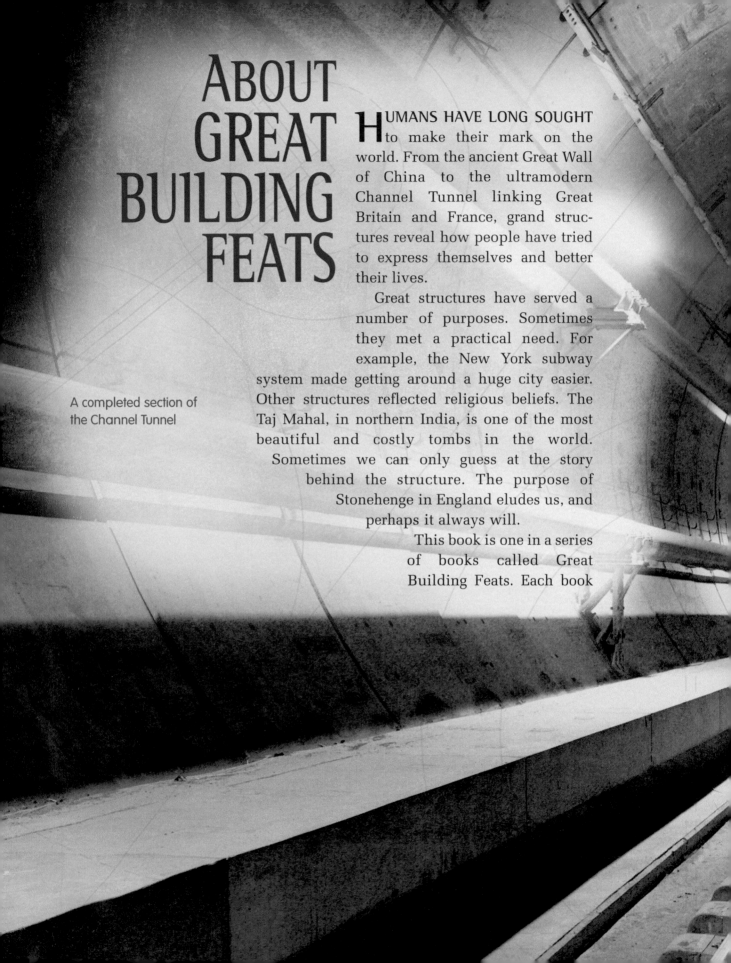

ABOUT GREAT BUILDING FEATS

A completed section of the Channel Tunnel

HUMANS HAVE LONG SOUGHT to make their mark on the world. From the ancient Great Wall of China to the ultramodern Channel Tunnel linking Great Britain and France, grand structures reveal how people have tried to express themselves and better their lives.

Great structures have served a number of purposes. Sometimes they met a practical need. For example, the New York subway system made getting around a huge city easier. Other structures reflected religious beliefs. The Taj Mahal, in northern India, is one of the most beautiful and costly tombs in the world. Sometimes we can only guess at the story behind the structure. The purpose of Stonehenge in England eludes us, and perhaps it always will.

This book is one in a series of books called Great Building Feats. Each book

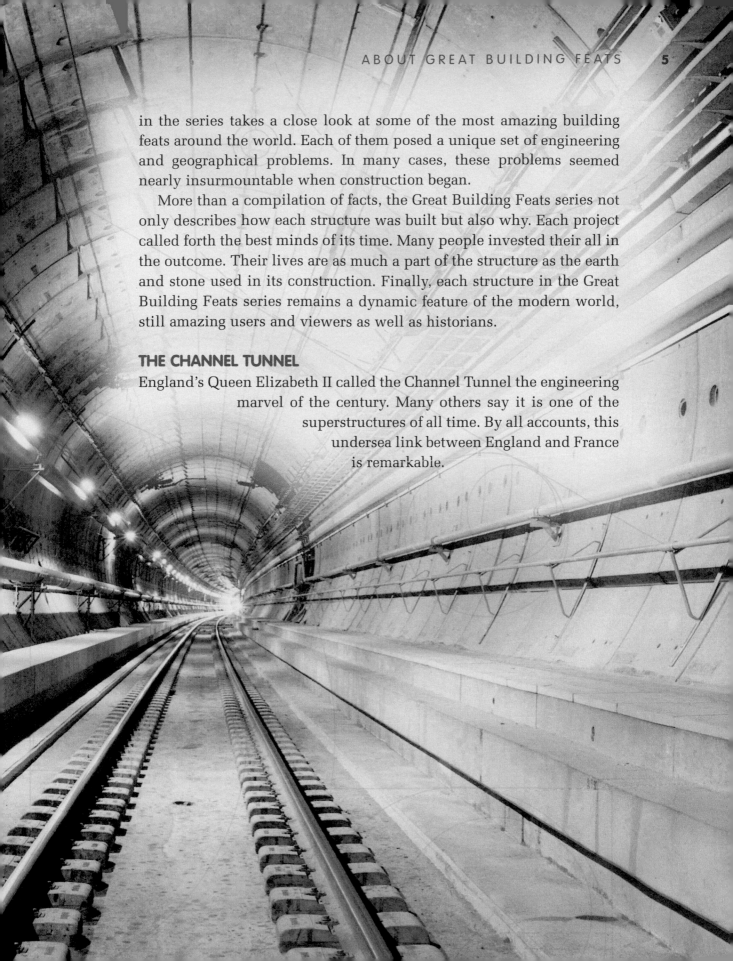

in the series takes a close look at some of the most amazing building feats around the world. Each of them posed a unique set of engineering and geographical problems. In many cases, these problems seemed nearly insurmountable when construction began.

More than a compilation of facts, the Great Building Feats series not only describes how each structure was built but also why. Each project called forth the best minds of its time. Many people invested their all in the outcome. Their lives are as much a part of the structure as the earth and stone used in its construction. Finally, each structure in the Great Building Feats series remains a dynamic feature of the modern world, still amazing users and viewers as well as historians.

THE CHANNEL TUNNEL

England's Queen Elizabeth II called the Channel Tunnel the engineering marvel of the century. Many others say it is one of the superstructures of all time. By all accounts, this undersea link between England and France is remarkable.

It is remarkable first because it took humans several centuries to join these two countries across the choppy waters of the English Channel. Emperor Napoleon of France first proposed a link in 1802. His and many subsequent plans were doomed by both the physical difficulties of the project as well as a deep reluctance by many Britons to see their country joined with the rest of Europe. It was not until the 1990s that the dreams of so many became a reality.

The Channel Tunnel, which runs from near Dover, England, to near Calais, France, is remarkable for other reasons as well. It is the world's longest undersea link. Although humans have been digging tunnels for many centuries, tunneling under water presents many complex problems. The sheer weight of the water surrounding the tunnel is an ever-present danger to workers. Throughout history many people have been crushed by the immense force of such water.

The geology of the English Channel presented its own challenges. Much chalk lies under the channel. The chalk is porous and easily water-soaked. This makes tunneling a difficult proposition. Engineers had to use their ingenuity to invent new methods of tunneling in order to be successful. One such innovation was a specially designed tunnel boring machine, able to slowly eat away at the rock while keeping the

A French geologist examines a rock formation at the beginning of tunnel construction.

water at bay. A special kind of waterproof coating for the tunnel walls also had to be invented.

Some of the world's finest engineers put their heads together to overcome the obstacles of spanning the English Channel under water. But during the more than seven years of construction, thousands of ordinary workers—most with no background in tunneling—had to rely on their own ingenuity to make the project a success. Along the way there were many setbacks. And, in the end, the project cost more than four times its original price tag. When the tunnel finally opened for business in 1994, however, it was a cause for celebration throughout Europe. More than 10 million people annually take the quick half-hour journey under the sea from England to France, or from France to England.

Much of the machinery used to create the Channel Tunnel, such as this enormous tunnel boring machine, was designed specifically for this project.

Chapter One
THE ENGLISH CHANNEL
(The Ice Age – 1975)

WITNESSES DESCRIBED IT AS "the handshake we've all been waiting for." A French worker named Phillippe Cozette had just extended his hand through a tiny opening in the rock more than one hundred feet (30 meters) beneath the English Channel. Grasping his hand from the other side of the small hole was an English worker named Graham Fagg. As soon as their hands clasped, crowds of workers on both sides of the hole cheered wildly. Hard hats waved in the air, and above the cheering came the sounds of champagne corks popping.

It certainly wasn't the first time a Frenchman and an Englishman had exchanged a handshake, but it was the first time that a handshake had occurred with each man technically standing in his own country. Just days earlier, a giant rock-eating machine had churned its way through the final inches of rock separating two tunnels, one coming from the French coast and one from the British coast of the English Channel. After centuries of isolation, Britain was united by land with the rest of Europe. The handshake between Cozette and Fagg symbolized the

Above, Phillippe Cozette and Graham Fagg make history on December 1, 1990, by reaching through the opening that connects two halves of the undersea tunnel linking England and France. *Right,* the English Channel is known for choppy waters and unpredictable weather. Humans have long sought an easy method of crossing it.

coming together of their two countries and a future of unity. But it also reflected the two countries' separate cultures and histories, which would continue to flourish. Although the two men had been chosen randomly in a lottery of all Channel Tunnel workers, they each represented their home country in a number of ways.

Phillippe Cozette was a construction worker from Peuplingues, France. This tiny village is about one kilometer (1.6 miles) from the site of what became the French entrance to the Channel Tunnel, so in 1986 Cozette went to apply for a job on the tunneling crew. Like many of his neighbors, he was excited by news of the tunnel project. But it was the prospect of a good, long-term job that excited him most. Jobs were hard to find in this part of France in the 1980s. Although Cozette had no experience tunneling, that did not bother the French construction managers. They would train most of their crew on the job.

Graham Fagg, on the other hand, had plenty of tunneling experience. In fact, he had traveled around the world as a tunneler. He had returned to England in 1986 partly for the novelty of working so close to home. The Channel Tunnel project was just one of many tunneling projects he would work on in his lifetime. While Cozette would later become a Channel Tunnel train driver once the passage was open, Fagg would find himself in a remote part of the world, helping to excavate ground for another tunnel.

The circumstances that led to their historic hand-shake took decades, even centuries, to develop. The body of water that separated England and France had long posed a great challenge to humans who wished to cross it. The hard labor and brilliant plans of a whole team of workers was finally coming together to achieve something that people had sought to do for as long as humans had lived in Europe.

AN ISLAND SEPARATED

Long ago, the island that became the country of England was connected by land to the rest of Europe. About a half million years ago, geologists believe, water from the North Sea overflowed and created what were later named the Strait of Dover and the English Channel. Since then, England has been an island sep-arated from the rest of the continent. The Channel has served as a barrier, separating England from France, Spain, Italy, and the rest of Europe.

Enemies have always had a hard time attacking England because of the Channel. Only two armies in

This centuries-old tapestry depicts William the Conqueror's voyage across the English Channel in 1066 on his way to invade England. William was one of the only invaders of England to successfully navigate an army across the Channel.

history have succeeded in crossing the Channel to invade the British Isles. The first was the Roman army around 54 B.C. The second was the army of William, Duke of Normandy, in A.D. 1066. For most of history, however, this body of water has protected Britain from invasion. The ships of the Spanish Armada were defeated in the Channel in the sixteenth century, and Emperor Napoleon of France was unable to make the crossing to conquer England in the nineteenth century. During World War II (1939–1945), most experts believe it was the difficulty of crossing the Channel that kept the German dictator Adolf Hitler from invading England.

The Channel has given the English a sense of identity. Throughout history the English have been proud to be separated from the rest of Europe. As British playwright William Shakespeare wrote, the Channel was like a "moate defensive . . . against the envy of less happier lands."

English people have long considered their culture to be more civilized than the cultures of the rest of Europe. The English author Tristan Jones wrote that when he first crossed the Channel, as a boy in the 1930s, he was forbidden to get off the ship in France because "it was the sort of place where men wore scent and played football on Sundays." Throughout the twentieth century, cartoons in English newspapers have made fun of French tastes, such as cooking with garlic. The French, in turn, criticize English food as having no flavor or elegance.

THE ENGLISH CHANNEL

The narrow body of water that separates England from France is actually an arm of the Atlantic Ocean. The French call the Channel La Manche (The Sleeve) because of its long, narrow shape. The Channel floor is generally flat and shallow, ranging from 150 to 400 feet (45 to 122 m) deep. The Channel is about 350 miles (560 km) long, and 150 miles (240 km) wide at its widest point, between Lyme Bay in England and the Gulf of St. Malo in France. It is 112 miles (180 km) wide at its west entrance, between Land's End, England, and the island of Ushant, France. At the east entrance, between Dover, England, and Cap Gris-Nez, France, it is 22 miles (34 km) wide. The Channel is dotted with islands, such as the Isle of Wight and the Channel Islands. The main Channel ports in England are Plymouth, Southampton, Portsmouth, and Dover. In France the main ports are Cherbourg, Le Havre, Dieppe, and Calais. The Channel is connected to the North Sea by the Strait of Dover. The North Sea separates England from Belgium and the Netherlands.

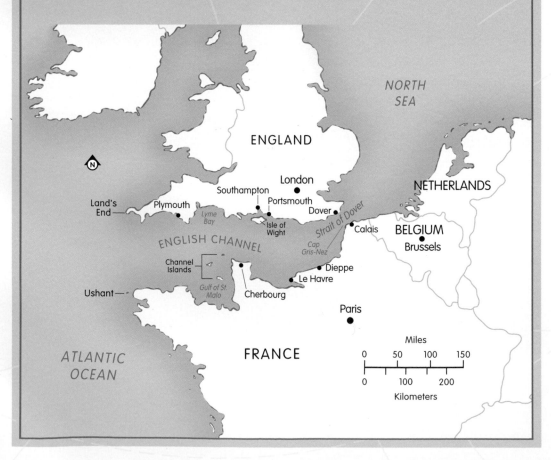

Despite the Channel's importance as a symbol of separation, people have long been fascinated with crossing it. In 1785 Jean-Pierre Blanchard and Dr. John Jeffries flew a hot-air balloon from Dover, on the English side of the Channel, to the French town of Calais. A few months later, two balloonists were killed when they tried to cross the Channel from France to England. In 1875 Mathew Webb was the first person to swim across the Channel. This body of water has also tantalized aviators. The first airplane crossing was made by a Frenchman named Louis Blériot in 1909. In 1979 Bryan Allen pedaled a propeller plane across the Channel in three hours.

William Shakepeare wrote about sending Henry V's army across the channel to make war with France in the 1400s:

And thence to France shall we convey you safe,
And bring you back, charming the narrow seas
To give you gentle pass.

In reality, however, the Channel has never been gentle to pass. Although at one point only 22 miles (35 km) separate England and France, the voyage across the Channel is notoriously difficult. This is mostly because of the choppy water and frequent bad weather in the area. Also, the Channel's bottom is lined with sand ridges that sometimes come as close as 10 feet (3 m) to the water's surface. With fast currents, dense fog, and a lack of safe harbors on either side, this body of water is extremely difficult to cross. For centuries stories have abounded about miserable crossings. British novelist Charles Dickens described a Channel crossing in the 1800s like this: "You . . . lay wretched on deck until you saw France lunging and surging at you." Other travelers described the decks of boats crossing the Channel as littered with seasick passengers. Nevertheless, people still made the crossing from England to France, or from France to England.

> "And thence to France shall we convey you safe, / And bring you back, charming the narrow seas / To give you gentle pass."
> —**William Shakespeare,** *Henry V*

Perhaps because of miserable boat crossings, people have been coming up with alternative plans for hundreds of years. Most of these plans

This British cartoon depicts Napoleon Bonaparte peering out over the English Channel and hatching a plan to cross it and invade Britain. Britons were wary of Bonaparte's proposed Channel link, fearful that the power-hungry French leader might use the tunnel he proposed to invade their country.

involved bridges or tunnels or a combination of both. One of the first recorded proposals for a tunnel was made to Napoleon Bonaparte in 1802. Napoleon, then the leader of France, said he was interested in improving communication and travel between England and France. He had a French engineer named Albert Mathieu draw up plans for a double tunnel. But the British government was worried about the potential of invasion from Napoleon or other European armies, and it would not agree to the plan. (Although the tunnel was never built, Mathieu's plan was very similar to the design of the tunnel that was finally completed almost two hundred years later.) In 1802 many people saw the idea as more fantastic than flying to the moon. And humans did manage to fly to the moon years before a tunnel was built.

A CHANNEL LINK

In the 1880s, a group of English and French people came up with a plan to build a tunnel underneath the English Channel. This time both the British and the French governments agreed to the idea. Digging began on both sides, using newly invented tunnel-boring machines. Working at a rate of about 328 feet (100 m) a week, the tunnelers expected to complete a tunnel in about five or six years.

It turned out to be emotions, not technology, that ended the project. Some English people were terrified of the possibility of European armies launching an invasion through the tunnel. Once these people began talking about their fears publicly, a strong anti-tunnel movement spread across the country. Supporters of the tunnel pointed out that it would put an end to the dreaded seasickness that accompanied a boat crossing. They also argued that the tunnel would make it much easier and

AIMÉ THOMÉ DE GAMOND

Throughout history, many people have become obsessed with the idea of linking England to France via the English Channel. Aimé Thomé de Gamond was arguably one of the more obsessed. Thomé de Gamond was a French engineer who first drew up plans for an iron-tube tunnel in 1834. During his lifetime, he came up with almost a dozen designs. Some involved bridges as well as tunnels. Some involved damming most of the English Channel. Others called for an artificial island to be built in the middle of the Channel. Many of his proposals were too fantastic to have ever worked, but he continued to draw new proposals and to try to find financial supporters for his ideas throughout his life. In all, he spent more than 175,000 French francs—a fortune in those days—on his dream of a Channel link. He died penniless in 1876.

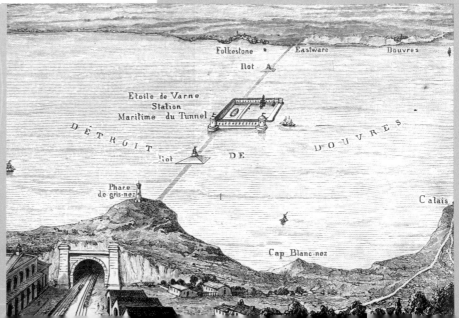

Aimé Thomé de Gamond created this plan for a Channel tunnel around 1850. It linked the British town of Eastware (between Folkestone and Dover) with Cap Gris-Nez in France and included an artificial island in the middle of the Channel.

more convenient to do business between the two countries. The fear of invasion won out, however, and in 1882 the British government refused to give its final approval to the project. The tunnel-boring machines had dug a total of 11,500 feet (3,500 m) of tunnel when the project was abandoned.

Since then, many other tunnel projects have come and gone. Throughout the twentieth century, companies in both England and France continued to submit tunnel proposals to their governments for approval. The idea tended to be more popular in France than in England. There were many reasons, besides invasion by a European army, that English people opposed a tunnel. One of these was the threat of animals with rabies crossing from Europe. Rabies is a disease carried by some mammals such as dogs, raccoons, and squirrels. A bite from a rabid animal can cause severe illness and even death in humans. Although rabies is widespread in most of Europe, there has not been a human case in Britain since 1902. English people were afraid a bridge or tunnel connection would make it easy for infected animals to slip through a tunnel and spread the disease to Great Britain.

Many people were against the idea of a tunnel or bridge crossing for economic reasons. Among the opposition were people who operated the ferries that carried passengers and vehicles across the Channel. Most of the ferries were owned by British companies. These companies were afraid they would lose all their business to the faster, easier method of crossing the Channel by tunnel or bridge. In fact, many of the ferry companies threatened to start a price war if a tunnel or bridge were ever built. This meant they would charge such low prices that almost everybody would choose to take the ferries instead of paying higher fees to take the bridge or tunnel. The bridge or tunnel, which would be very expensive to build, would likely go out of business.

In the 1950s, a group of American and French lawyers and business-people made a major step forward. They convinced banks and private businesses around the world to invest in a tunnel project. This was an important move because it meant that the French and British govern-ments would not have to pay for the project. The group was able to raise a good deal of money. But this time, the French and British govern-ments were in the middle of an argument about whether Britain should join the Common Market, an economic association of European coun-tries to which France belonged. Britain wanted to join, but France was against the idea. Britain would not agree to the tunnel unless France

A worker emerges from the doorway of the Channel Tunnel begun in 1973 at St.-Margaret's-at-Cliffe near Dover.

agreed that it could join the Common Market. In the end, the tunnel project was not approved. Many years later, in 1973, Britain did join the Common Market (known by that time as the European Economic Community).

The year 1973 also marked the only time since the 1880s that any actual construction was begun on a tunnel across the Channel. This time both the British and the French governments were in favor of the project. Unfortunately, the timing was poor. Britain was in the middle of a very difficult period of high unemployment and rising inflation. The British government didn't have enough money for new ventures. By 1975 it had backed out of the deal. Only a hole one-half-mile long near Dover had been dug.

Chapter Two
A Channel Link Competition
(1984–1986)

Above, In 1984 French president François Mitterrand and British prime minister Margaret Thatcher signed an agreement stating that their countries would work together to create a cross-Channel link. *Right,* Shakespeare Cliff was chosen to be the site of the English tunnel end.

For decades people on both sides of the Channel had their hopes raised about linking England and the rest of Europe, only to have them dashed again for one reason or another. Then in 1984, Prime Minister Margaret Thatcher of Britain and President François Mitterrand of France made a stunning announcement: "A fixed cross-Channel link would be in the mutual interests of both countries," they wrote in a joint statement.

These may seem like mild words, but to the many people dedicated to achieving this cross-Channel link, they were music to the ears. It was not all that surprising that the French government was interested in building a bridge or tunnel across the Channel. After all, people in France had been in favor of the idea for almost two hundred years. But it was quite surprising that Prime Minister Thatcher was ready to commit the British government to the project. For decades, the British government and much of the public had been against a Channel link.

In the mid-1980s, the British government was particularly opposed to the
idea for economic reasons. Like much
of the rest of the world at the time, the
British economy was going through
rough times and did not have funds for
such a massive project. So Prime
Minister Thatcher and President
Mitterrand came up with a creative
solution. When the two leaders
announced their commitment to a
Channel link, they had one stipulation:
no government money could be used.
That is, people who wanted to build a
bridge or tunnel had to be able to raise
enough money or borrow enough from
banks and other businesses to pay for
their own project.

This meant the government
wouldn't lose any money on the
projects, and, depending on how
big the winning project was, there

would be many new jobs. Most of these jobs would be in construction. Since both France and Britain had high unemployment at the time, the new jobs would be very valuable. They might help lift the countries out of their economic troubles. Not only would the governments have to pay less in unemployment benefits, they would receive more money in taxes from people with new jobs.

Then, in April 1985, the two leaders made another stunning announcement: There would be a competition for the best Channel link plan. Construction companies were asked to submit a description of the type of link they proposed to build (either a bridge, a tunnel, or a combination of the two), how long it would take to build it, and how much money it would cost. A committee set up by the two countries would then pick a winner.

The governments wanted to move quickly. They set the deadline for entries for October 31, less than seven months away. That gave companies very little time to put together thorough proposals. The governments promised that by January 1986, they would either pick one of the proposals as a winner, or reject them all. Thatcher said that building a high-speed Channel crossing was "something our generation can perhaps do for future generations."

THE PROPOSALS

Once they announced the competition, groups in both France and Britain began scrambling to come up with a plan. One of these groups was Balfour Beatty Construction, a big British company that had built huge structures in all parts of the world. Balfour called in its head engineer, Gordon Crighton, to prepare the proposal. Crighton, a burly man in his mid-fifties, had spent most of his life in the heavy-construction industry. He was as smart about business as he was about the hands-on work, although he preferred jeans

> "[Building a high-speed Channel crossing is] something our generation can perhaps do for future generations."
>
> —**Prime Minister Margaret Thatcher**

and a hard hat to a suit. Crighton had worked at Balfour for five years in Nigeria, Peru, the Philippines, and Hong Kong, among other places. In 1985 he was working on a subway system in China and returned to England to help with the proposal. He was back in China within a few months. He knew that there had been many previous plans to build a Channel link, and he knew that none of them ever came to much. He was not expecting this time to be any different.

Balfour was not the only company interested in winning the competition. Many engineers around the world were scrambling to come up with a design. By October, proposals began pouring in to the review committee. Some involved a tunnel, some involved a bridge. Generally, a plan for a tunnel meant trains would carry cars and people through the tunnels. Since any tunnel would have to be almost 30 miles (48 km) long, cars wouldn't be able to drive through. The exhaust from the cars, which contained poisonous carbon monoxide, would build up in the closed space. If there were a bridge or a bridge-and-tunnel combination, people would be able to drive their own cars between the two countries.

Some of the proposals were very complex, and all would take many years to build. One plan was submitted by a group of four Englishmen, who called their plan the Eurolink. The Eurolink would be a bridge that would carry both cars and trains across the Channel. Hydroelectric generators would be placed along the supports of the bridge. The generators are huge machines that use water to make electric power. The plan was to sell the power to both Britain and France to pay for the bridge. This way, the designers said, travelers using the bridge would not have to pay anything.

Another plan, the "Brubble," called for both a bridge and a tunnel. The tunnel would carry trains between Dover and Calais. The bridge would be a huge plastic tube suspended from eight towers built across the Channel. The tube would have several decks for cars to drive across, and the plastic would shield the drivers from bad weather. But critics said that having a bridge across the entire Channel would be too dangerous. They said that too many large ships travel through the Channel, and they might crash into a bridge. Also this proposal was one of the most expensive. It was expected to cost $7 billion.

The "Brunnel" was another plan, and many people thought it was the best. It featured a bridge and tunnel combination. Drivers would drive their cars on a bridge that would extend 5 miles (8 km) out into the Channel, where an artificial island would be built. At the island, the cars would drive down a spiral ramp to a 13-mile (21 km) tunnel. At the end of the tunnel would be another ramp, another island, and another bridge 5 miles (9 km) off the French coast. There would also be a separate, parallel tunnel for trains that would run the whole 23 miles (37 km) under the Channel. The promoters of this plan said it would give freedom of choice to Channel crossers. One reason that the Brunnel appealed to people was that travelers could drive their own vehicles. This plan would have cost about the same as the Brubble, about $7 billion.

The other plan that seemed to stand a chance in the competition was the "Chunnel" proposal that Gordon Crighton had designed for Balfour Beatty Construction. This plan called for two parallel railroad tunnels with a service tunnel running in between them. With its two parallel tunnels, it was very similar to two earlier plans—one proposed by Napoleon in 1802 and one begun and abandoned in the 1970s. In the Chunnel, electric trains would carry cars and trucks at high speed

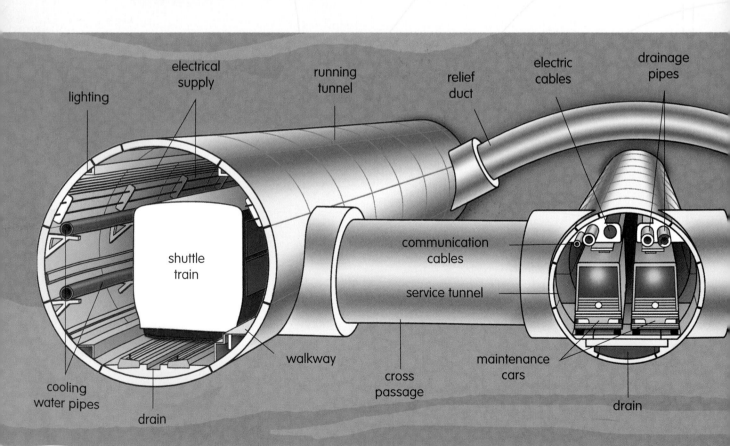

between France and England. The crossing would take just under one-half hour. Its designers said that with a train leaving about every five minutes, they could transport 4,300 vehicles per hour. While this plan was perhaps not as ambitious as the Brunnel proposal, with its artificial islands and freedom of choice for travelers, it would cost much less. The proposed cost was $3.6 billion.

A WINNING DESIGN

On January 20, 1986, the creators of the Eurolink, the Brunnel, the Brubble, and the Chunnel plans gathered in the small city of Lille, France. By afternoon, they would know which design had been chosen.

THE CHUNNEL DESIGN

The proposed Chunnel project would be one of the largest engineering projects ever undertaken in the world, and yet the design was actually quite simple. The Chunnel would consist of three tubes dug through the chalk 131 feet (40 m) below the floor of the English Channel. The two outside tubes would be 24 feet (7 m) in diameter. Railroad cars would travel through these tubes, carrying passengers, cars, and trucks. The middle tube, only 15 feet (5 m) in diameter, would be used by workers to access the travel tunnels for repairs, service, and emergencies. The tunnels would be 31 miles (50 km) long, with 23 miles (37 km) under water.

Specially designed double-decker rail cars would transport automobiles under the Channel, and single-deck cars would hold trucks. High-speed passenger trains would use the tunnel in trips between London and Paris. The journey would take about half an hour, forty-five minutes less than it takes a ferry to make the crossing. Officials said they could load an entire train in about ten minutes, and the tunnel could accommodate more than one thousand vehicles per hour going each way.

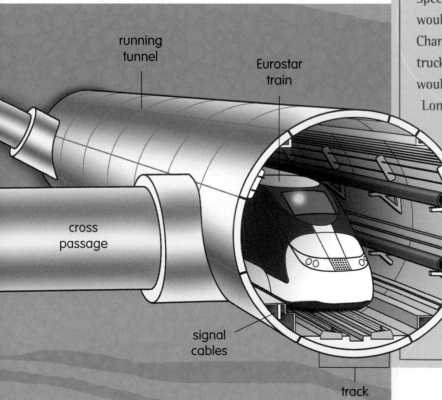

running tunnel

Eurostar train

cross passage

signal cables

track

Prime Minister Margaret Thatcher and President François Mitterrand met in Lille on January 20, 1986, to announce that the concession to build and operate the Channel Tunnel had been granted to the Channel Tunnel Group/France Manche.

The streets were filled with children waving tiny British and French flags. A band played the national anthem of Britain, "God Save the Queen," followed by the national anthem of France, "La Marseillaise." One day earlier, newspapers in France and Britain had leaked that the Chunnel project was going to be the winner. Still, nobody knew for certain.

The city's town hall was draped in the flags of both countries for the momentous occasion. Representatives from all of the groups that had submitted plans crowded into the room. Prime Minister Thatcher declared, "It is a great day. Today means we are embarking with determination to build this link. It is not only the link itself. It means something symbolic between Britain and France."

Mitterrand added, "This is an act not only of goodwill but a grand and grandiose vision which will provide great benefits for our people. France is very happy."

Then came the announcement everyone had been waiting for: the Chunnel, officially called Eurotunnel, had won. Balfour Beatty Construction was just one of a number of French and British companies that joined together in a newly formed group to design, build, and pay for the Chunnel. The group was called Channel Tunnel Group/France Manche. Before long, the name of the company would be shortened to Eurotunnel.

But winning the competition was just the first of many difficult tasks faced by Eurotunnel before construction could begin on the Chunnel. In the first place, the proposal had been thrown together in just under seven months and was not very detailed. There was still plenty to work out, including big questions. Where was the money going to come from? Where were they going to find enough talented people to work on such a huge project? Would the British and French governments give their official approval to the more detailed plans? And, finally, how were they ever going to tunnel through 30 miles (48 km) of chalk at the bottom of the English Channel?

A DISLIKE OF TRAINS

During the competition for a Channel link, many people believed that British Prime Minister Margaret Thatcher preferred the proposals that involved bridges to those, like the Chunnel, that had only tunnels. This was because people could drive themselves over a bridge, while in a tunnel, cars and trucks would have to be loaded onto a train. Thatcher did not particularly care for trains. She once called British Rail, the government-sponsored railroad company, "a colossal waste of money."

Thatcher's dislike of trains was reflected a few years later, when the British government refused to pay for a high-speed train link from London to the Channel Tunnel terminal at Folkestone. The French government built more than 200 miles (320 km) of train tracks to enable high-speed trains to whisk passengers from Paris to the tunnel in record time. Having equally high-speed trains on the British side was necessary to meet Eurotunnel's goal of moving people from Paris to London in three hours. By the mid-1990s, when Thatcher was no longer Prime Minister, high-speed tracks were finally begun in England.

Chapter Three
GETTING STARTED
(1986–1987)

Construction begins in Calais, France, in 1987.

THE YEAR 1986 WAS A BUSY one for Eurotunnel. After all, winning the competition simply meant that they had permission from Britain and France to build a Channel tunnel. It was up to the Eurotunnel executives and engineers to complete the designs, raise the money, and begin construction on this massive project. Sir Nicholas Henderson was the company's chairperson. It was his job to recruit the right people for the project. This meant finding the world's best engineers, as well as people who could convince other people to invest money in the project. Collecting enough money to get the project under way was the first task for Eurotunnel.

Since Henderson had once been the British ambassador to both the United States and France, he knew a lot of people who had money and who might be persuaded to invest in the Channel Tunnel. The project was estimated to cost about $3.6 billion ($5.7 billion once inflation and interest charges were added in), so Henderson had a lot of convincing to do. Eurotunnel began selling stock in the company at $6 a share. People had to have a lot of faith to invest in a project that wasn't even started, but many people were optimistic about the plan and bought shares of its stock. They hoped that in ten or twenty years they would be able to sell their Eurotunnel shares of stock for huge profits. Eurotunnel used the money from the sales of the stock to help finance the Channel Tunnel project. Another way that Eurotunnel raised funds was by convincing banks to lend money for the project. Many banks were nervous about lending money for such a risky undertaking. Several earlier attempts to build a tunnel had failed. In the end, however, Henderson and his colleagues were able to convince enough banks to lend them the money they needed to get the project going.

Raising money was not the only obstacle Eurotunnel faced. The company also had to work out all the details of the Chunnel design. Since a tunnel of this magnitude had never been constructed, this was no small task. The company hunted around the world for the best engineers, but it was hard to convince top engineers to work on a long, risky project like the Channel Tunnel. For one thing, most engineers were used to projects that lasted for two or three years. Then they moved on to another part of the world to begin a new project.

They were not excited about spending seven or more years working beneath the English Channel.

One of the first engineers that Eurotunnel signed up for the project was Gordon Crighton, who had helped with the original plans the previous year. After the plans had been submitted, Crighton had returned to China, to the subway project he was working on there. In October 1986, his company called him back to London. Crighton was not at all eager to join the Channel Tunnel project: "I got back on the Saturday, and went into the office on the Monday, and was told I'd be on the Channel Tunnel the next Monday," he later recalled. "I said, 'I am not going to take something that is going to last seven or eight years. I am not going.'" Plus, he added, he didn't want to be digging "a long boring hole" under the Channel. However, Crighton, like many other reluctant people, could not stay away from the challenge of one of the world's greatest engineering projects.

Once enough talented people were hired, these people had to answer some very difficult technical questions. Foremost among these questions was how it would be possible to cut through 30 miles (56 km) of rock under the sea. A machine that could do this job safely didn't even exist. It would have to be invented before any work could begin. The dangers of working this far beneath the sea were immense. The water above weighed about 7,000 tons (6,349 metric tons). The force of this water rushing into one crack or leak in the rock could crush both workers and machines.

To build a machine to cut through the rock, Eurotunnel turned to the Robbins Company, a tunneling-machine manufacturer near Seattle,

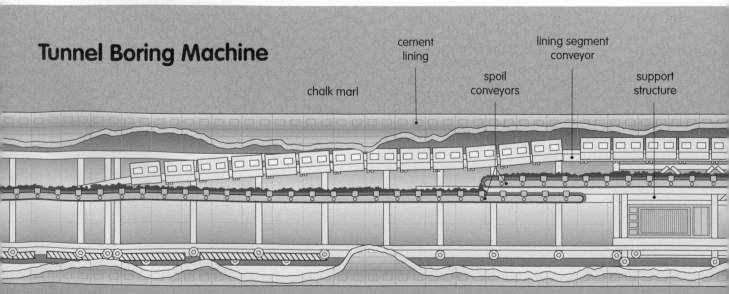

Tunnel Boring Machine

cement lining

lining segment conveyor

chalk marl

spoil conveyors

support structure

Washington. Robbins had built some of the world's strongest and most complicated tunneling equipment. The company began work to create a machine for the Channel Tunnel project. The result was a giant snakelike monster called a tunnel boring machine, or TBM. A TBM is more than 8,000 feet (2,400 m) long and weighs more than 15,000 tons (13,605 metric tons). It can have a rotating head that is 50 feet (15 m) in diameter. Along this head are hundreds of cutting edges. These teeth are made of tungsten carbide, the strongest material known to humans. An engine pushes the giant snake forward and drives the cutterhead through the rock. The millions of tons of excess rock (spoil) that are dug up are transported back on conveyer belts through the body of the machine. In all, the Robbins Company built eleven TBMs for the Channel Tunnel project.

The job of tunneling through the chalk rock on the English side of the Channel was relatively straightforward. But on the French side, many tiny cracks in the rock made the job twice as difficult. The machine

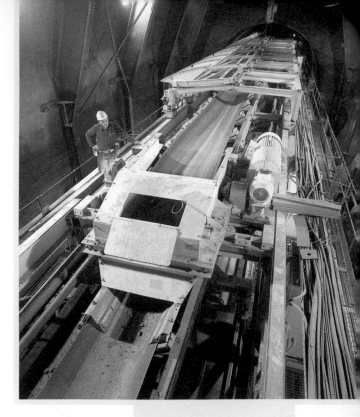

Above, This overhead spoil conveyor from the TBM transports excavated rock to wagons, which carry it to the surface for disposal. *Below,* The various working parts of the TBMs used to dig the Channel Tunnel can be seen in this detailed diagram.

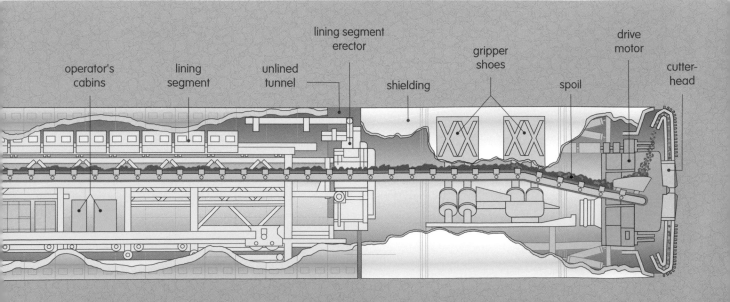

operator's cabins | lining segment | unlined tunnel | lining segment erector | shielding | gripper shoes | spoil | drive motor | cutter-head

CHALK MARL

The floor of the English Channel is lined with thick layers of chalk. Scientists divide it into three layers: the Lower, Middle, and Upper Chalks. The first two layers, the Upper and Middle, are very porous, which means water can easily flow through them. For this reason, these layers are very difficult to tunnel into. The Lower Chalk, however, is actually a mixture of chalk and clay called chalk marl. Clay is extremely waterproof, so when it is mixed with chalk in the chalk marl, it forms a perfect material for tunneling. Because the chalk marl is still about 60 percent chalk, it is easy to cut through but strong enough to stand without support.

On the British side of the English Channel, the Lower Chalk is about 260 feet (80 m) thick. This provided the perfect spot for the tunnel. But on the French side of the Channel, the chalk marl layer thins to about 210 feet (65 m), and it extends farther down under the sea—too deep to put the tunnel. This geology would present the tunnelers with one of their first big problems: they would need a machine that could withstand the pressure of the water that would leak in when it cut through the soft Middle Chalk layer on the French side.

working here would have to be able to stand up to twice as much pressure as any tunneling machine had ever had to before. For this, the people at Robbins developed a special machine that was half TBM and half submarine. The French workers would soon begin calling her Brigitte.

BREAKING GROUND

One cold, dark morning in December 1987, a group of men stood shivering near a massive hole in the ground in Folkestone, England. Located just beneath a large chalk overhang called Shakespeare Cliff, the hole was the site of the abandoned 1974 attempt to dig a tunnel beneath the English Channel. Thirteen years later, Eurotunnel was going to begin its own project from the same spot. Using the one-half mile (1-km) entrance shaft, or opening, that had been dug in 1974, the real work of tunneling down deep enough to cross the Channel at the chalk marl level could begin.

The first order of business was to get the TBMs in place to do their work. Since they were so huge, they could not just be moved to the end of the shaft where work would begin. Instead, they had to be taken apart and lowered piece by piece into the shaft. The workers descended along with the machines. Each worker was aware of the historic

The TBMs were taken apart and reassembled below ground. Here, tunnelers work on putting together the cutterhead for the French TBM.

nature of the moment. Many had been fascinated since they were young by the idea of a tunnel under the English Channel. But they all understood the dangers involved in working on such a project. One false step or miscalculation could lead to serious injury or death for hundreds of workers.

One of the greatest challenges was having French and British people working so closely together. Although the two countries are separated by only 21 miles (34 km) of sea, their cultures are quite different. For one thing, engineers are trained differently in each country. Sir Alastair Morton, the Eurotunnel chairperson, explained it this way: "A French engineer is trained to make a plan. They can't start work until they can see what is to be done, see where their task fits into the whole thing, and see how it's all going to be organized as it goes along." In contrast, Morton said, the British prefer less planning and more working. "British culture is to sit down and say, 'Now what have we got to do, chaps?' and get to work." To build the Chunnel, these two different engineering styles would have to work together.

In addition, the French and British have always been rivals. For the Eurotunnel project, this meant that the French would want the project to be more French, while the British would want it to be more British. In this situation, Gordon Crighton was an ideal leader because he was Scottish. Since Scotland is part of Great Britain, the British workers were happy to have a British person heading the engineering team. But since Scotland isn't England, the French were also happy to have a Scot in charge. After all, Mary Queen of Scots had once been the French queen, and the Scottish had at one time joined the French to fight against England.

SHAKESPEARE CLIFF

The construction site in England was located at Shakespeare Cliff, along the Channel coast about 5 miles (8 km) from the village of Folkestone. The closest city to Shakespeare Cliff is Dover. There were actually two different sites at Shakespeare Cliff—the upper site, on top of the cliff, and the lower site, at sea level. The upper site held offices for engineers and crew managers and was connected to the lower site by a 360-foot (110-m) shaft. Elevators in this shaft carried people and small supplies back and forth. Large equipment was transported through a narrow road tunnel, dug during the 1974 tunnel project. This tunnel connected the two sites. At the lower site, two small sloping tunnels, also dug in 1974, were used for moving materials, equipment, and workers in and out of the main tunnels. Spoil, the chalk and clay that was drilled out of the seabed to make the tunnels, was also brought out through these work tunnels.

Construction on three tunnels began at the lower site, stretching under the Channel toward France. From the opposite direction, workers would drill toward Folkestone, where the train terminal for entering the tunnel would be located.

Construction at the Shakespeare Cliff site took place around the clock.

A complete ring of reinforced concrete lining segments mounted on a special pallet is lowered down the huge French access shaft at Sangatte.

SANGATTE

The French construction site was located in the tiny village of Sangatte, on the Channel coast about 2 miles (3 km) from the town of Coquelles. The closest city to Sangatte is Calais.

At Sangatte, a huge vertical shaft was built from ground level to where the tunneling began, about 230 feet (70 m) underground. The shaft was 180 feet (55 m) in diameter. All materials, equipment, people, and spoil moved in and out of the tunnels through this shaft.

The tunnels stretched out under the Channel toward England in one direction and inland toward the town of Coquelles in the other direction, where the French train terminal would eventually be built.

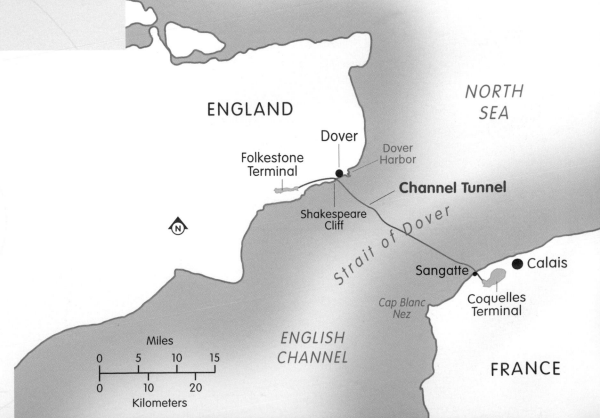

Chapter Four
TUNNELING
(1987 – 1990)

ONCE THE WORKERS AND THE equipment were in place, it was time to get started. Working from both sides of the Channel, the middle service tunnel would be dug first. Then the two outside tunnels would be constructed. The first task was to reassemble the TBMs, which had been lowered into the shaft in parts. The massive front cutterhead had to be connected to the service train, which held the hydraulic engine to power the huge machine. The service train also held the conveyor belts that would carry out the debris. Working at full speed, the TBMs would be able to clear about 750 feet (230 m) of rock per day. This would produce about 24,000 tons (22,000 metric tons) of waste an hour. Rock eaten by the cutting edge was taken to disposal sites in both England and France.

As the TBMs slowly snaked their way beneath the Channel, workers lined the sides of the tunnel with concrete slabs. In all, one-half million slabs of concrete would line the walls of the Channel Tunnel. Because of the immense pressure of the water bearing down on the tunnel, a special kind of concrete had to be used. This concrete was even stronger than the kind used in nuclear power plants. To manufacture this concrete, special factories were built in both England and France. The concrete was reinforced with steel rods, since the pressure it would have to withstand would be twelve times the pressure felt on the earth's surface. When the concrete slabs were

Above, Tunnelers work on assembling the TBM that would excavate the rail tunnel. *Right,* A TBM, ready for action

finished, they were transported to the front of the TBMs. As the TBM's cutterhead ate through the rock under the sea, operators fit the concrete and steel walls right behind. Then they filled in the tiny spaces with cement grout. Each ring of tunnel wall weighs 40 tons (36 metric tons).

For most of 1988, two teams worked steadily on the middle service tunnel. The French team began at Coquelles, France, and worked its way west toward England. The British team started at Folkestone, England, and snaked slowly east. The TBMs roared as they chewed through the earth toward each other. Gordon Crighton oversaw the British part of operations from his office, high on Shakespeare Cliff. Meanwhile, the French engineer, Laurent Leblond, helped to guide Brigitte from his office at the Coquelles

WATER, WATER EVERYWHERE

Tunneling underwater presented engineers with complex problems. Since a certain amount of water was bound to seep into the newly created tunnel, all electrical pipes and other cables had to be waterproofed. It was easy enough to deal with a small amount of water seepage. The real danger was that at any moment the tunnel walls could give way to the enormous pressure of the surrounding sea. To prepare for this possibility, the tunneling crews were equipped with two long hoses with pumping equipment. This equipment was capable of pumping fast enough to allow the workers to reach safety in the event of a flood.

Another serious problem caused by water is called overbreak. Overbreak occurs when the water-soaked layers of rock surrounding the tunnel start to break apart and fall into the newly dug tunnel. The crew inside a TBM was protected by the massive machine from these falling chunks of rock. But for workers outside the TBM, the chunks posed imminent danger.

construction site. The two TBMs would, it was hoped, meet up in the middle of the Channel in about one year.

In the early months of 1988, everything was on schedule. Then the first real problem reared its head. The waterproofing seal designed to protect the TBMs from the salty seawater was not working. The French TBM, Brigitte, was silent, stopped dead in her tracks. The problem was that the seal was allowing seawater to leak onto the metal of the machine, and the water's heavy concentration of salt was eating away at the metal. It seemed like a fairly simple problem. But executives at Eurotunnel were worried that it could put the whole project in jeopardy. "One thing we all understood was that it would be very hard to restart the project if it got stopped," Chairman Morton recalled later. "The relationships with the banks, problems with the contractors, difficulties with the government, or just plain difficulties of whatever kind would bring an end to the project."

Luckily engineers were able to fix the problems of Brigitte's waterproofing seal. They developed a new seal made of paper and a special kind of grease. When the paper gets wet, it expands and creates a permanent, completely waterproof seal. Soon Brigitte was back at work, but the project was by then nine months behind schedule. Both teams would have to work extra hard to try to make up time.

Keeping the machines on course was one of the most complicated issues of the whole project. Most tunnelers use a high-tech satellite mapping system to chart the route of a tunnel. But the Chunnel was too far underwater for even the most high-tech system to work. Excellent mapping was essential. If the French and British teams were off by even a tiny distance, they wouldn't meet up as planned in the middle of the Channel. Then the whole project would be a failure. So the engineers developed a space-age laser guidance system. A red laser on the cutterhead of each TBM sent a beam of light forward. This beam hit a control point that told the computers on board the service train behind the cutterhead how to stay on course. A small drill bit about 2.5 inches wide (60 mm wide), connected to the front end of the TBM, drilled a path for the large machine to follow. Using this system, the two TBMs, one snaking its way from France and one from England, would, it was hoped, be able to meet up in the center of the English Channel.

An engineer checks the laser guidance system to ensure the TBMs remain on their planned path.

Muck wagons carry spoil excavated by the tunnel boring machine to the surface for disposal.

FRENCH SPOIL

The chalk under the French side of the Channel was very wet and difficult to tunnel through. The spoil was very hard to dispose of as well. To make for easier disposal, workers mixed the watery spoil with more water to make it entirely liquid. Railcars then transported the spoil out of the tunnel to the shafts, where it was pumped up to a huge reservoir disposal site at Fond Pignon, France. The yogurtlike liquid spoil eventually hardened into a chalky layer 131 feet (40 m) thick.

By New Year's Day 1989, things seemed to be running smoothly, though the project was costing a lot more money than Eurotunnel had estimated. The earlier problems with the TBMs seemed to be solved, and all the machines were working as fast as they could. In fact, one TBM even set a world record for tunneling speed.

Then, on January 20, 1989, tragedy struck. Nineteen-year-old Andrew McKenna, an engineering assistant, was crushed to death by a service train carrying debris out of the tunnel. Apparently McKenna hadn't heard the train coming. This was the first death in three years of work on the Channel Tunnel. It affected all the workers. As they mourned their colleague's death, they were reminded of just how dangerous their jobs were. Before the tunnel was completed, eleven more workers would lose their lives.

Life on the tunneling project was difficult in many ways besides the ever-present sense of danger. There was the day-to-day fact of being underground for ten-hour shifts for several years. Many times the workers would arrive early in the morning while it was still dark outside. They often wouldn't leave until it was dark in the evening. They might not see daylight for six or seven days in a row. Working in such a tight space also affected many people. Some workers said they had never been claustrophobic (afraid of enclosed spaces) before. But working in the tunnel changed that. "You could be down working in 3 feet [1 m] of water, with nowhere else to go," explained a construction worker named Michael Dix. "It was dark, it could be dusty, and that could be very claustrophobic."

HELEN NATTRASS

The Channel Tunnel project was mostly a men's club, with few women involved. Occupations like tunneler, engineer, and geologist (a scientist who studies rock formations) tended to attract mostly men. Men were also more attracted to the vagabond lifestyle that went along with tunneling projects. As a female geologist, Helen Nattrass was familiar with being one of the only women at many jobs. The Chunnel project was no exception. A tough supervisor, she won the respect of the thirty male geologists who worked for her.

SUCCESSFUL MEETING

October 30, 1990, was particularly tense for the engineers working on the Chunnel. This was the day that the two tunnel-digging machines were scheduled to meet. All that remained were 330 feet (100 m) of earth between the two tunnels. After decades of planning and three solid years of work, England and France would finally be connected under water—if everything went as planned. People on both sides of the Channel waited expectantly to hear the news that the project was successful. Only the engineers knew that there was a chance the two machines might not meet up at all. If they did not, the entire project could be ruined.

In France, Chief Engineer Laurent Leblond had guided the French TBM, Brigitte, almost to the middle of the Channel. Brigitte had

An engineer on the British TBM talks to his French counterpart in the French undersea service tunnel as the moment of breakthrough approaches.

finished all but the last few hundred feet of her work.

Meanwhile, in England, Gordon Crighton was in charge of the British side of the project. Having completed its half of the tunnel just days earlier, the British machine was silent, just 330 feet (100 m) from where Brigitte continued her journey. The drill bit had bored its narrow hole ahead of the British machine, reaching toward Brigitte. The plan was for Brigitte to continue eating her way through the rock until she met the drill hole. At that point, the tiny hole would connect the two halves.

But Crighton and Leblond knew they could not take the meeting of Brigitte and the drill hole for granted. They had each worked for three years to make sure that the two halves of the tunnel would join. Both engineers were among the best in their field and had plenty of experience planning tunnels. They knew that though they had done everything they could to make sure the two holes met, there was the grim chance that they could be off by many feet. It was extremely difficult to plan the course of the TBMs in the rocks, and it was even harder to make sure the machines followed the planned course. If the two sides were off by more than 8 feet (2.5 m), it would mean a delay of more than a year and a cost of millions of dollars. The engineers' reputations would be ruined. They waited nervously.

Down in the French side of the tunnel, Steve Cargo was also nervous. He was an Englishman who was working with the French to connect Brigitte with the drill hole. Cargo was known by his coworkers as "the snail," because all of his equipment had "S. Cargo" on it, which sounded the same as the French word for snail, *escargot*. Cargo knew from experience that drill holes often do not go where they're supposed to in such heavy rock.

From the other side, the British threaded a long, thin rod called a drill probe through the hole. If everything had been calculated correctly, Brigitte would run straight into the drill probe. Cargo talked to the engineers on the British side by telephone, as Brigitte inched closer to where the probe was supposed to come out. "I can't see anything," he told them.

The workers did not lose hope. The British told Cargo to drive Brigitte another foot. Brigitte dug her way forward, and after a few minutes Cargo got back on the telephone. He still could not see the drill probe, but he saw water flowing through a hole in the rock straight ahead of him. The British team pulled back the probe and sent it through the hole again. This time Cargo saw it, directly in front of him.

"I've got it!" he yelled into the phone. England and France were linked. Steve Cargo removed the end of the drill probe to keep as a souvenir of the historic moment.

A French engineer, inside the cutterhead of the French TBM, grips the probe drill sent from the approaching British TBM to check the accuracy of the alignment of the two tunnels.

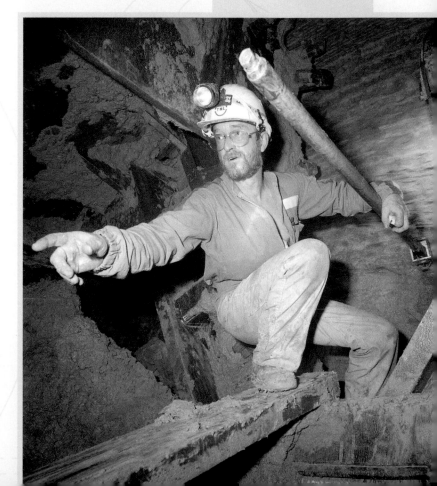

Chapter Five
FINAL DETAILS
(1990–1993)

NEWS THAT THE PROBE HAD made it from the British side of the tunnel to the French side traveled quickly throughout the construction site. Mud-caked tunnelers threw their hard hats up in the air. Engineers popped champagne corks. The probe showed that the two holes were off course by about 20 inches (51 cm), but this was a small enough distance that the engineers could easily work with it. On December 1, the official celebration, including the famous handshake between Phillippe Cossette and Graham Fagg, took place.

Workers didn't pause long for celebration, however. Although the completion of the center tunnel was indeed a success, there was still plenty of work to be done. There were still two more tunnels to be dug, as well as the crossover links.

Before work could begin on the two main tunnels, the giant machines that had created the center hole had to be removed. They were now stranded in the middle of the tunnel, miles under the sea, and they could not back up. This meant they would have to be taken apart and slowly removed from the tunnel, piece by piece. But this would be a very expensive operation, and the project already was costing more than anyone had imagined. The engineers came up with a creative solution. They would turn one of the tunneling machines slightly off the course of the tunnel and "bury" it in the chalk rock at the bottom of the Channel. Then the other TBM could drive forward out of the tunnel. The British machine was selected to be buried. After it was driven into the rock, it was sealed off, and the tunnel wall was covered with its

Above, French and British tunnelers celebrate the historic breakthrough in the service tunnel on December 1, 1990. *Right,* A tunneler hand-trims a tunnel wall with a jackhammer following excavation by the TBM.

concrete slab. Then Brigitte snaked her way to the English coast, where she could be easily recovered.

Soon the tunnelers were hard at work on the two main tunnels. Since these were the tubes through which the large passenger trains would carry people and vehicles, they were wider than the center service tunnel, which only had to carry service trains. The running tunnels, as the outside tubes were called, would be 25 feet (7.6 m) in diameter. That's exactly 50 percent wider than the inner service tunnel. There would also be two sets of large crossover links to join the tunnels. These links, running from one tunnel to the other, would allow the trains to switch from one set of tracks to another. The workers called the crossover links

PISTON RELIEF DUCTS

The two main tunnels of the Channel Tunnel are connected every 820 feet (250 m) by piston relief ducts. These tubular passages arch over the service tunnel, in the center of the running tunnels. They are called relief ducts because they relieve the extra air pressure caused by a train's high speed. As a train speeds through a tunnel, it pushes the air ahead of it. Air pressure increases as all this air builds up in a small space. The piston relief ducts allow air to escape into the other running tunnel. Tunnelers cut all of these relief passages by hand, with tools called air spades. These are extremely noisy hand chisels that slowly chipped away the chalk and rock to create the passages.

cathedrals because they were so massive, 40 feet (12 m) high and more than 500 feet (152 m) long. They were the largest undersea caverns ever built.

SAFETY PRECAUTIONS

Safety in the completed Channel Tunnel was one of the main issues that engineers had to consider during construction. Natural disasters were a big concern. What would happen to travelers in the Channel Tunnel during a fire or earthquake? The tunnel had to be protected against terrorist acts, too, such as bomb threats.

Engineers made the tunnel as safe as they could. Giant steel doors, covered with flame-resistant material, separated the crossover caverns from the tunnels. This would ensure that if a fire did break out it would not spread easily. To allow passengers and crew to escape from fire or other calamities, special emergency walkways were added in the center service tunnel. During construction, special evacuation teams practiced emergency procedures, like fire drills and bomb-threat evacuations. Everyone at the Eurotunnel company knew that safety was critical to the tunnel's success.

Planners soon realized that the French and the British had quite different views on how to handle safety precautions. Eurotunnel's chairman Morton explained: "There are two different philosophies. The French have a belief in intelligent operators using sophisticated equipment, but being in charge of the equipment. The British have a culture of fail-safe computers." In other words, the British tended to rely on computers, while the French used a more hands-on approach.

"The Chunnel is a [combination] of both," Morton said. "You can be quite sure, whichever you think is better, that the Chunnel's got it."

The result of combining the French and British approaches to safety is an extraordinarily safe tunnel. "No other tunnel in the world is as safe as this one, with the fire-supply systems, emergency walkways, and all the procedures put in place to cover every eventuality," said Richard Storer, building and infrastructure manager for Eurotunnel. Engineers on the project had tried to plan for any possible threat to the safety of the passengers, the crew, and even the equipment inside this magnificent tunnel.

FINAL DIGGING

By the spring of 1991, the TBMs had almost completed their work. On May 22 of that year, two TBMs met in the middle of the northern running tunnel. This is the tunnel that carries passengers from England to France. About a month later, on June 28, a huge crowd gathered in the southern tunnel to watch the French TBM complete its last few yards of work and join up with the hole dug by the British machine. Approximately four years after digging had begun, the last tunnel was complete.

This little hole represents the breakthrough that linked the two halves of the northern running tunnel.

Together the three main tunnels and nine smaller entrance tunnels added up to about 90 miles (145 km) of tunnel. The amount of debris removed to make the tunnels, about 80 acres (32 hectares), could fill sixty-eight football fields. There was champagne and cheering in the crowd as the final tunnel was completed. But then there was a strange silence. The giant machines were shut off, and the last one was about to be dismantled and carted out of the third tunnel.

Workers sharing the excitement also thought how strange the silence was. Many of them had descended into the tunnel to work six days a week, fifty weeks a year, for four years. Their workday had been defined by the darkness of the shaft and the roar of the TBMs. They could not believe they would not be hearing that roar any longer. As they celebrated, they already felt nostalgic for the time they had spent working under the English Channel.

Tunnelers celebrate the last breakthrough ceremony on the Channel Tunnel project after the TBM completed its drive on the south rail tunnel.

THE TRAINS

The celebration did not go on for long. There was plenty of work to be done before the tunnels were ready for travel. There were finishing touches to be put on the tunnels and on the two cross-chambers that connected them. The tracks needed to be laid for the trains. It would be another two years before the thirteen thousand workers were finished with their jobs and the Channel Tunnel would be open for business.

Much of the important final work was going on in factories across Europe. This was where the trains that would transport people and vehicles through the tunnels were being designed and assembled. Seventeen of these trains were under construction before the tunnel was even built. Nine were to transport passenger vehicles, and

> ## EUROSTAR TRAINS
> Eurotrains—the trains that would carry cars and trucks through the Channel Tunnel—were built by and would be operated by Eurotunnel itself. Passenger service through the tunnel would be offered by the British and French railways—British Rail and SNCF (Société Nationale des Chemins de Fer Français). For this passenger service, other special trains, called Eurostar trains, were built. Eurostar trains travel between London and Paris, and between London and Brussels, Belgium. Each train has 18 cars and can carry 766 passengers. On land they can reach speeds up to 186 miles per hour (300 km/h) on special high-speed tracks. In the tunnel, they can travel up to 100 miles per hour (160 km/h).

eight would carry freight in heavy trucks. Each train would have a locomotive, or engine car, at each end. Four spare locomotives were built, for a total of thirty-eight.

The trains were especially designed to meet many challenges presented by tunnel travel. For one thing, each end of each train would need a locomotive. Unlike most trains, trains traveling through the Channel Tunnel would need to travel in both directions. When a train arrived in one country, it would unload and reload in the terminal. Then it would head back in the opposite direction on the other track. The designers estimated that each train would make about twenty trips a day. Because of this, the locomotives would have to be extremely strong—able to pull the heavy trains at 87 miles per hour (140 km/h) up the steep slopes at each end of the tunnel. The trains also had to be able to deal with drastic and sudden changes in temperature. For instance, it might be freezing at the aboveground terminals, where freight and passengers

Shuttle trains are assembled in a plant in Britain for future use in the Channel Tunnel.

boarded, but in the tunnel it still would be hot and humid. All of these conditions presented challenges to the train designers.

Eurotunnel's great attention to safety matters added other challenges to the design of the locomotives. It was most important that a stalled train not get stranded in the tunnel. So in case the front locomotive broke down, the rear locomotive had to be able to start up and push the train to its destination. Since all eastbound trains rode on one track and all westbound trains on another, a stalled train would have to complete its journey in the same direction it started. Also, if a train broke down completely—if neither of its locomotives could work—then the next train to come along would have to be strong enough to push the stalled train to the station. These locomotives would be the most powerful in the world. Powered by electricity sent through overhead cables in the tunnels, they would have one hundred times the power of the average car.

To make sure the trains were working properly, test runs were conducted on train tracks throughout Europe. Most of the tests went well, but one unexpected problem was discovered: the running trains produced an enormous amount of heat. The temperatures around the test tracks rose to 140 degrees Fahrenheit (60 degrees Celsius). This would be dangerously hot inside the cavernous tunnel. Once again engineers were called upon to come up with a fast solution to a big problem. They created a pipeline inside the tunnels with cold water moving through it. These cold pipes would absorb the heat like a sponge. When the water became warm from absorbing the heat, it would be pumped out to cooling stations on either shore. There the water would be chilled again and recirculated through the pipeline.

With this cooling system in place, the Channel Tunnel was ready to accommodate the high-powered locomotives. A driver and a captain would be in charge of each trip. The driver would sit on the left side at the very front of the locomotive. Although there are large windows in front of the driver's seat, there is really nothing to see inside the tunnel. Instead, the drivers use a complex control panel to operate the train. This panel includes dozens of knobs and levers as well as a large screen that displays information such as the train's speed and position.

Fast-speed train drivers often suffer from a condition called "segment flicker." This happens when a series of similar objects rush by the side of a train and cause the driver to get sleepy or even drift off to sleep. To prevent this, there are no side windows on the locomotives.

The driver in the Eurotrain can operate the controls either sitting or standing. In France, most train drivers sit at the controls, but in Britain they often stand. Since Eurotrain operators come from Britain as well as France, the cabs are built to be comfortable for both.

The seat to the right of the driver's is for the train's captain, who would not often sit here. Instead the captain would sit in the train's rear locomotive. The captain is in charge of dealing with any emergency on the train. There are two screens at the captain's seat that can be switched to any of the many closed-circuit cameras located throughout the train. The captain would be able to make announcements during trips and get important messages to passengers and crew. Captains would have to be prepared to drive the train, if for some reason it had to be pushed out of the tunnel. If this happened, the captain would switch to the left seat and become the driver. Then the original driver would become the captain for the rest of the trip.

EUROTRAIN CONTROLS

Eurotrain drivers have four main controls located on an instrument panel, called the driver's console, at the front of the locomotive. On the right side of the console is the power controller. This can be set on either forward or reverse. The driver pushes it forward to make the train move faster in either direction. Pulling backward on this control applies a special kind of brake that stops the train from gaining speed when it is going downhill. The main brake control is on the left side of the console. The driver uses this to reduce the speed of the train. This control automatically shares the braking between the locomotive's brake system and the train's brake system. All the way to the left is a lever that applies only the locomotive's air brakes. The driver uses this when the locomotive is running on its own, without the train attached.

Chapter Six:
UP AND RUNNING
(1993 – 1997)

A train driver's eye view from inside the Eurostar train as it approaches the entrance at Coquelles

BY THE END OF 1993, THE tunnel was ready to be tested. People had dreamed for hundreds of years about connecting England to France, and finally the moment was here. Thousands of people had worked for more than six years building the tunnel. Eleven tunnelers had lost their lives. Workers had overcome many setbacks, and problems with the giant TBMs had been corrected. The project ended up costing far more than originally expected, but the Eurotunnel company had somehow made it all come together. The tunnels were completed, the tracks were laid, and the trains were ready. On December 10, 1993, the first train would make the long-awaited journey.

Four hundred invitations had been sent out. They were sent to people who had worked for Eurotunnel as well as to other top business people—two hundred in France and two hundred in Britain. The British guests would ride a train from England, through the Channel Tunnel, to the French terminal at Coquelles. The French guests would board a train in Paris and take a round-trip ride through the new tunnel. The trip also would end in Coquelles. At the terminal in Coquelles, a huge tent was set up for a celebration. There would be a choir, gourmet food, and champagne. Then a ceremony would mark the "handover"—the day when all work on the Channel Tunnel would be completed.

Although the event had been planned for months, there were enough last-minute problems to make the people at Eurotunnel extremely nervous. Although all work on the project had been completed, the British government would not allow its brand-new, high-speed Eurostar train to make the trip, because the train had not yet been tested to meet safety requirements. The ceremony guests would have to travel on an ordinary first-class passenger train from London to Folkestone. Then they would have to switch to a different train for the journey through the tunnel because the first-class train could not run on the kind of overhead power used in the tunnel. For this portion of the trip, an ordinary British Rail train was used. To make matters worse, the substitute train was much narrower than the Eurostar train for which the tunnel had been designed. This meant that the passengers had to use a temporary bridge to board the narrower train at the tunnel terminal in Folkestone.

Despite these annoyances, the historical first journey went forward. The two hundred British guests arrived at the Victoria train station in London by 2 P.M. on December 10. Twenty minutes later, the train

Passengers on the very first Channel Tunnel voyage in 1993 await the boarding call at the Coquelles Terminal in France.

roared out of the station toward the Channel Tunnel terminal at Folkestone. Guests sat in their train seats, toasting the success of the day with champagne. At 4:00 P.M., the celebrity-loaded train pulled into the Folkestone terminal. Then there was a two-hour delay as they waited for the train from France to make the round-trip through the tunnel. As a safety precaution, only one train at a time was allowed in the tunnel on this day. Finally, at just after 6:00 P.M., the British train descended into the tunnel. As the train zoomed through miles of tube, passengers could see only a blur of gray wall with the white stripe of the cooling pipe running down the middle. Twenty-two minutes later, the tunnel wall disappeared, and the Coquelles terminal came into view. Two hundred train passengers had just experienced one of the world's most historic journeys. As the train doors opened, a band greeted the arrivals with a famous British traveling song, "It's a Long Way to Tipperary."

The British passengers got off and joined a group of French travelers, who had returned half an hour earlier from their own tunnel journey, under a huge tent. More champagne, fireworks, music, and food marked the occasion. By 8:30 P.M. London time (9:30 P.M. French time), the British guests were back onboard their train for the twenty-two minute return trip to the Folkestone station.

OPEN FOR BUSINESS

Nearly six months later, Britain's Queen Elizabeth II and French president François Mitterrand marked the official opening of the Channel

Tunnel. On May 6, 1994, the queen boarded a Eurostar luxury train in London. She was met a few hours later in Coquelles, France, by President Mitterrand. The two cut a huge symbolic ribbon at the terminal in Coquelles. The queen paid tribute to the fifteen thousand workers who had toiled for seven years on the project, as she said, "for the benefit of all humanity."

President Mitterrand also praised the workers. "We now have a land frontier," he said. "This work, full of imagination and invention, shows what France and Britain can do when they put together their talent, energy and resources. We can achieve even greater things, so let us vow to do more for the cause of Europe." Soon the two world leaders climbed into the queen's burgundy Rolls Royce. They drove onto the freight platform and onto Le Shuttle, the train that carried passenger cars, for a trip back to England. Half an hour later, they were on British soil.

The queen of England, *center*, and other dignitaries on the platform at Coquelles, after the ribbon-cutting ceremony

By the summer of 1994, the Channel Tunnel was open for business. The construction project had lasted seven years and had cost far more than expected. The final price tag on the project was more than $16 billion, and some people added it up to be more than $21 billion. The Eurotunnel company would be in debt for years before the tunnel ever earned a profit. The company's goal was to have one-third of the 18.5 million travelers who annually crossed the Channel—until then, either by ferry or by plane—use the new tunnel in 1995.

From opening day, tourists and business travelers alike were attracted to the newest method of Channel crossing. Channel Tunnel passengers have a choice of two ways to travel between England and France. With a car, they can drive to the terminal in Folkestone, England, or in Coquelles, France, and drive right on to Eurotunnel's Le Shuttle trains. These trains have twenty-eight cars that can carry up to five automobiles on each of their twin decks, or about 280 automobiles per train. Special train cars are available for larger vehicles. Passengers can either stay in their vehicles or stretch out in the train cars, which have rest rooms. The journey takes about thirty minutes, plus another thirty for loading and unloading. The journey on one of the ferries that makes the same trip takes about an hour and a half. But speed is not the only advantage of

Individual cars enter the ferry complex through a series of tollbooths and ramps.

the Channel Tunnel. Since Le Shuttle trains are underground, they avoid the notoriously foul weather of the Channel. This weather not only brings on seasickness in travelers but often results in delayed or canceled trips.

The other Channel Tunnel option, for travelers without cars, is to take the high-speed Eurostar trains between London and Paris. The Eurostars make the London-to-Paris or Paris-to-London trip in three hours, nineteen minutes of which is spent in the tunnel. A London-to-Brussels trip is also possible in three hours and fifteen minutes. While an airplane flight between London and Paris is only one hour, travel to the airport and check-in procedures add to travel time. Many travelers would rather be seated comfortably for three hours than spend it rushing around airports, so Eurostar has lured away about fifty percent of the airlines' business between the two cities.

In Eurotunnel's first two years of operation, everything seemed to run smoothly. There was enough passenger demand between London and Paris for the railways to schedule trains every hour between the two cities. Before Eurotunnel and the high-speed Eurostar, a train trip between London and Paris took twelve hours, including the ferry. When the trip was reduced to one-quarter of that time, it attracted many more tourists and business travelers. In 1996 between 60 and 70 percent of all passengers between England and France were riding Eurostar trains. Eurotrain shuttles, which run

Inside the Le Shuttle trains, passengers may stay in their vehicles or walk around in their train car.

The Channel Tunnel was almost instantly successful. Thousands of passengers took the quick undersea trip each day.

on demand for drive-up passengers, continued to fill up quickly. About one-half of all automobiles traveling between Dover and Calais were taking the shuttle trains through the tunnel in 1996, and almost 40 percent of trucks were using the undersea route. Eurotunnel still owed billions of dollars to its investors, but it was beginning to earn profits from customers. Disaster was the last thing from anyone's mind.

FIRE IN THE TUNNEL

Jeff Waghorn, a truck driver, said he first smelled smoke when his main course arrived. It was November 18, 1996, and Waghorn was having dinner with several other truck drivers in the dining car of a shuttle train. With their trucks loaded onto the cargo railcars, the truck drivers were headed from France to England through the Channel Tunnel's south tube. Soon after Waghorn smelled the smoke, he said, a steward rushed in to warn them of a fire in the tunnel. Waghorn said they all raced to a rear door, and the steward opened it to see what was happening. Smoke was pouring in from the tunnel, so they quickly closed the door.

Fire in the Channel Tunnel was one of the worst nightmares that could be imagined. The designers and builders had carefully installed top-notch equipment. Tunnel and train staff practiced evacuation routines regularly. On this November evening, more than two years after the tunnel had opened for business, all of these safety precautions were going to be tested.

Inside the dining car, it was pandemonium. "Some people were saying, 'Let's get out,'" Waghorn remembered. "But the steward said we couldn't because the smoke was worse outside than inside." Instead, the steward told everyone to lie on the floor, cover their faces with wet napkins, and remain calm until help arrived. Less than twenty minutes later, Waghorn said, French firefighters arrived and led the truck drivers to safety in the center service tunnel. The giant doors designed to keep fire out of the service tunnel had done their job: the tunnel was smoke-free. In the service tunnel, the passengers and crew could be treated for smoke inhalation. Then they boarded a Le Shuttle train in the north tunnel for the trip back to Coquelles. They arrived in the French terminal at 11:24 P.M., about one and one-half hours after they had left for the trip to England. Of the thirty-four people onboard the train, only two needed to be hospitalized for smoke inhalation, and they were soon released.

It was a huge relief to everyone that no one was seriously injured. It meant that the safety precautions had been successful. The question of how the fire started still remained to be answered. Investigators learned that the fire had begun on one of the twenty-nine trucks being transported on the train's cargo cars. It broke out just as the train was pulling out of the French terminal, and it quickly spread to five other trucks. As it spread,

> "Some people were saying, 'Let's get out.' But the steward said we couldn't because the smoke was worse outside than inside."
>
> **—Jeff Waghorn**

it ignited the railcars and their brake fluid. Although passengers and crew were evacuated quickly, it was not until the following morning that firefighters had the flames extinguished.

The damage caused by the fire was enormous. The temperature in the tunnel had reached 2,700 degrees Fahrenheit (1,482 degrees Celsius). Steel, concrete, cable, train, and trucks had all melted. Fifteen of the twenty trucks onboard had been damaged. More than 600 yards (550 m) of the tunnel were destroyed. Burned and broken chunks of concrete were all that remained along this long section. Firefighters said it looked like an abandoned coal mine, with broken pipes and cables hanging from the ceiling. It took 140 workers more than six months to complete the repairs, which cost more than $80 million. They had to reline the tunnel walls with concrete, install new tracks, and

This truck was one of many damaged by the intense heat in the tunnel fire.

A crew visits the tunnel after the fire to assess the damage.

completely replace the cooling pipes, the power supply, and the phone wires used for communicating with trains.

While the extensive repairs were under way, much was back to normal within a few weeks of the fire. The north tunnel, which carries trains from England to France, was never damaged. Once the damaged section was sealed off in the south tunnel, traffic from France to England resumed. The trains simply crossed over to the north tunnel to avoid the closed portion.

Although the fire had certainly been a catastrophe, many people were reassured by the fact that the evacuation went smoothly and no lives were lost. Soon after the fire, a survey showed that about two-thirds of British people and three-fourths of French people thought the tunnel was safe. "The accident has already happened," passenger David Lloyd told a newspaper reporter at the time. "That means there won't be another one, not in our lifetime. And everyone got out okay. You couldn't say that about many plane crashes, could you?" Indeed, it seemed that the smooth evacuation process after the fire had eased many travelers' minds about the tunnel crossing. Soon, as many people were traveling through the tunnel as before the fire.

Chapter Seven
THE CHANNEL TUNNEL
(1998–Present)

Right, shortly after the fire, passengers and freight companies were once again using the Channel Tunnel regularly.

IN MARCH 2001, A MAN NAMED Omar sat near his bed in a Red Cross shelter in France. Omar was a thirty-year-old Iranian man who had left his own country to escape poverty. In Iran, he could not afford to feed his family. There were no jobs, and food and clothing were scarce. He left his family in Iran and traveled to Europe. He traveled by walking and by hitchhiking. He made his way across Europe and hoped to make it through the Channel Tunnel to England. In England he thought he could find a job and send for his family.

In Sangatte, France, Omar joined thousands of other refugees from poor countries such as Iran, Afghanistan, Russia, and the Czech Republic. Most European countries

have laws against people immigrating without permission. Since many refugees don't have jobs or money, they are usually denied permission to enter those countries. But the refugees feel they have nothing to lose since they see no hope of finding a job or feeding their families in their own countries. Many of them try to make it to England, where asylum laws are less strict. There, they either find work or try to make their way to the United States or Canada.

Refugees gather in Sangatte because it is the closest town to the Coquelles terminal for the Channel Tunnel trains. Their goal is to sneak through the Channel Tunnel into England. It is not easy to do. Every night the refugees try to get onto a shuttle train without anyone seeing them. Sometimes they jump from bridges onto trucks that are going to drive onto a Eurotrain shuttle. Someone may jump in front of a train headed for the tunnel in order to slow it down so other refugees can jump onto it. In the winter of 2000–2001, when Omar was trying to get through the tunnel, security guards caught 150 to 200 people a night trying to cross. Omar told a newspaper reporter that he had tried 41 times in three months.

It is very dangerous to try to get through the tunnel illegally. Once, guards found nine immigrants from Romania hiding underneath a high-speed passenger train. The temperature was nearly freezing, and the immigrants had a three-year-old girl with them who almost died. Another time guards found a man from Iraq who had died after getting stuck between the underside of a train and the train platform. But the

Refugees wait for a bus in Sangatte to go to Coquelles, where they will attempt to enter England illegally via the Channel Tunnel.

refugees feel it is worth the danger. When the refugees are caught by the guards, they are released into the town of Sangatte. Then they try again the next night.

So many refugees were living in Sangatte that the Red Cross eventually built a shelter for them. The shelter was about 1.2 miles (2 km) from Eurotunnel's Coquelles terminal. It was in the giant warehouse that Eurotunnel used to store concrete during the tunnel's construction. The warehouse was full of hundreds of cots on which the refugees slept. The walls were covered with posters warning of the dangers of trying to sneak into England through the Channel Tunnel. In 2001, the shelter held up to 1,200 people a night. The Red Cross said the shelter was necessary because the refugees needed a place to sleep and get food. They said that if the shelter was not there, the refugees would still stay in Sangatte, but they would have to sleep on the streets.

Eurotunnel has to pay a fine to the British government every time an immigrant stows away on one of its trains. This law is aimed at trying to get companies to help the government crack down on illegal immigration. Eurotunnel pointed out that they have to pay these fines, but the French government had done little to prevent the refugees from coming to Sangatte. Eurotunnel officials felt that the shelter encouraged refugees to come to Sangatte to try to cross through the tunnel. So, at the request of Eurotunnel, the French government shut down the shelter in early 2002.

Eurotunnel has spent more than $4 million trying to prevent stowaways on their trains. They have more than 100 night security guards and more than 200 cameras at the terminal. They have barbed wire, floodlights, and electric fencing surrounding it. French police also patrol the area with dogs. Still, even without the shelter, desperate people continue to try to make it through the tunnel to England.

THE CHANNEL TUNNEL'S FUTURE

Within its first few years of operation, the Channel Tunnel became an integral part of Europe. Problems that affect Europe will no doubt continue to affect the tunnel. Illegal immigration remains a big issue in many parts of Europe. The Eurotunnel company will have to pay attention to this issue for many years to come.

FOILED IRA PLOT

Terrorism has long been a threat in Europe. Long before Americans became familiar with the potential for terrorist acts of destruction, Europeans were living under this threat. In England the Irish Republican Army (IRA) has existed as a threat to public safety for decades. Northern Ireland is under British rule, and IRA members want it returned to Ireland. To protest the presence of British soldiers in Northern Ireland, the IRA plotted and carried out terrorist acts throughout England and Northern Ireland on many occasions. Often they planted bombs in public places, like busy London streets and department stores, where they have killed many Britons.

In the late 1990s, the IRA plotted to blow up a section of the Channel Tunnel. It was going to be the biggest terrorist act ever on British soil. Luckily British police found out about the plot and were able to stop it. One terrorist was killed and five others were arrested. British police found 10 tons of explosives, rifles, handguns, and ammunition that were to be used to destroy the tunnel. Since then there has been no serious terrorist threat in the Channel Tunnel.

FOLKESTONE RAIL CONTROL CENTRE

All operations in the Channel Tunnel are monitored from a state-of-the-art Rail Control Centre at the Folkestone terminal *(above)*. This giant room sits at the rear of the terminal, partially below ground. Controllers sit at three curved rows of desks, in front of a giant electronic diagram of the entire Channel Tunnel system.

Controllers at the Folkestone center are responsible for rail traffic at this terminal as well as all operations throughout the rest of the tunnel. Since much of the tunnel's operations are automatic, the controllers' real duty is to monitor information to ensure everything is running smoothly and to be able to make quick decisions in the event of an emergency. For instance, all trains are controlled by an electronic signaling system that relays information to the control center. This enables controllers to see that all trains are on course and that the system is working. Controllers are also responsible for monitoring the tunnel's ventilation, drainage, and power supply.

An identical control center was built at the Coquelles terminal to be ready to take over from the one at Folkestone, if necessary. So far it has never been put to such emergency use. It is used only for monitoring the rail traffic in and out of the Coquelles terminal.

Many other challenges have to be faced as well. Some of these are the very issues that made people originally opposed to the idea of a Channel link. One of these is the threat of rabies entering into Britain. For many years, people were not allowed to bring any animals, including their pet dogs and cats, into Britain unless they put them in quarantine for six months. Animals in quarantine are kept separate from all other animals to make sure they are not carrying a disease. Before the Channel Tunnel was even open, people began worrying that animals, like mice or foxes, would be able to carry the rabies virus through the tunnel from France to Britain. To prevent this, the Channel Tunnel's designers covered every opening with steel mesh to keep animals out. They also placed electronic fences throughout the tunnel. So far, these measures have been successful in keeping rabies out of Britain. In the last few years, pet dogs and cats have even been allowed to travel back and forth under certain special circumstances. In 2000, the first year of this project, more than 12,000 pets traveled through the tunnel.

The Channel Tunnel continues to attract more and more travelers. In its first six years, almost 60 million people—more than the entire population of Great Britain—passed through the tunnel. In 2000 alone, about 3 million cars, 1 million trucks, 80,000 buses, and 7 million train passengers used the tunnel. Also in 2000, 12 percent of all foreigners who visited Great Britain used the Channel Tunnel, and 10 percent of all Britons traveling abroad used the undersea link. Although the company has a huge debt, Eurotunnel's goal is to cover expenses by 2028. As part of its original contract with the British and French governments, Eurotunnel plans to unveil a proposal for a drive-through tunnel for motorists by 2012. With the opening of such a tunnel, travelers would truly have a full range of options for travel between England and France—options that seemed like a mere dream for hundreds of years.

A Timeline of the Channel Tunnel

1802 Albert Mathieu designs a tunnel under the Channel for Napoleon. Britain won't agree to it.

1880s Work on a tunnel is begun using new tunnel-boring machines. Britain again objects.

1950s Investment is sought for the Channel Tunnel. Britain backs out when France refuses to agree to admit Britain into the Common Market organization.

1973 Britain and France agree on terms, and construction is begun on a tunnel.

1975 Britian pulls out of the agreement due to financial difficulties.

1984 Prime Minister Margaret Thatcher of Britain and President François Mitterrand of France announce interest in a Channel link between the two countries.

1985 A call goes out for designs for Channel link competition.

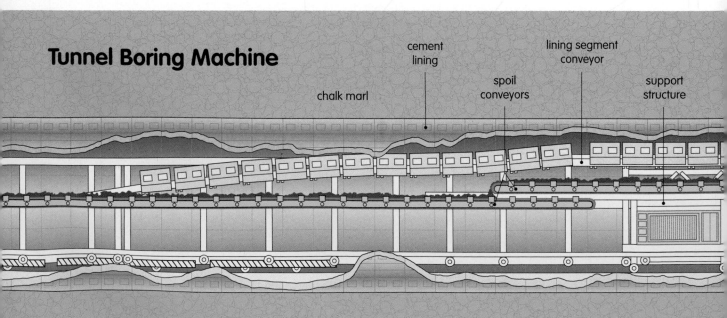

Tunnel Boring Machine

chalk marl

cement lining

spoil conveyors

lining segment conveyor

support structure

1986 Eurotunnel's design for the Chunnel is chosen.

1987 Ground is broken for the Channel Tunnel.

1990 Steve Cargo, drilling for the French team, runs into British drill probe. France and Britain are linked.

1991 Drilling of north and south passenger tunnels is completed.

1993 First trainloads of dignitaries ride through the tunnel to celebrate in France.

1994 The Channel Tunnel officially opens.

1996 Fire in the south tube!

2000 Three million cars, 1 million trucks, 80,000 buses, and 7 million train passengers use the Channel Tunnel.

2002 Eurotunnel reduces its Channel Tunnel debt by $704 million.

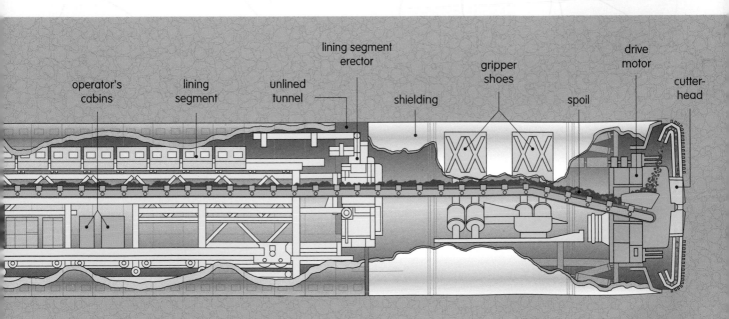

Source Notes

pp. 4, 5, 12, 13, 18, 20, as quoted in Fetherston, Drew, *The Chunnel: The Amazing Story of the Undersea Crossing of the English Channel* (New York: Random House, 1997); p. 9, as quoted in DeYoung, Karen. "Britain, France Close Bids for Chunnel, or Perhaps Brunnel," *Washington Post*, 1 November 1985; p.11, as quoted in Sancton, Thomas A. "Hands Below the Sea: Britain and France Sign a Pact for a Cross-Channel Train Tunnel," *Time*, 3 February 1986; pp. 14, 16, 17, 22; p. 27, as quoted in Drozdiak, William. "Plight at End of Tunnel: Chunnel Formally Opens Among Fears that Debt, Fares May Sink The Marvel," *Washington Post*, 7 May 1994; p. 28, as quoted in Barbash, Fred. "Fire Revives Fears on Chunnel Safety," *Washington Post*, 20 November 1996; p. 29, as quoted in Barbash, Fred. "Eurotunnel Inches Back on Track: Crews Work to Repair Fire-Damaged Shaft," *Washington Post*, 24 January 1997.

Selected Bibliography

Barbash, Fred. "Channel Tunnel Fire Repairs Could Top $100 Million," *Washington Post*, 3 December 1996.

————. "Eurotunnel Inches Back on Track: Crews Work to Repair Fire-Damaged Shaft," *Washington Post*, 24 January 1997.

————. "Fire Revives Fears on Chunnel Safety," *Washington Post*, 20 November 1996.

Daley, Suzanne. "Chunnel's Human Traffic Has a Dream," *New York Times*, 15 March 2001.

DeYoung, Karen. "Britain, France Close Bids for Chunnel, or Perhaps Brunnel," *Washington Post*, 1 November 1985.

Drozdiak, William. "Plight at End of Tunnel: Chunnel Formally Opens Among Fears that Debt, Fares May Sink The Marvel," *Washington Post,* 7 May 1994.

Fetherston, Drew. *The Chunnel: The Amazing Story of the Undersea Crossing of the English Channel.* New York: Random House, 1997.

Hawkes, Nigel. *New Technology: Structures and Buildings.* New York: Twenty-First Century Books, 1994.

Lyall, Sarah. "Channel Tunnel Service Returning to Normal," *New York Times*, 29 December 1996.

Redman, Christopher. "An Island No More: Hello! Allo!" *Time*, 12 November 1990.

Sancton, Thomas A. "Hands Below the Sea: Britain and France Sign a Pact for a Cross-Channel Train Tunnel," *Time*, 3 February 1986.

Semmens, Peter, and Yves Machefert-Tassin. *Channel Tunnel Trains*. Folkestone, U.K.: Eurotunnel Press, 1994.

Superstructures of the World: Eurotunnel. Unipix Entertainment Inc. and WOW TV for The Learning Channel, 1998.

Timberlake, Cotton. "The Chunnel Half Done, Over Budget," *Washington Post*, 21 July 1990.

Wilkinson, Philip. *DK Inside Guides: Superstructures*. New York: DK Publishing, 1996.

Yenckel, James T. "Fearless Traveler: Making the Leap: The Chunnel and Beyond," *Washington Post*, 11 August 1996.

Further Reading and Websites

Hawkes, Nigel. *Structures and Buildings*. New York: Twenty-First Century Books, 1994.
This book discusses the engineerng and building details of several world-famous structures, including tunnels and skyscrapers. It contains color illustrations and diagrams of many fascinating building feats.

Newman, Cathy. "The Light at the End of the Chunnel" *National Geographic,* vol. 185, no. 5 (May 1994), pp 37–47.
The article describes how the Channel Tunnel will change the cultures of France and England. It is illustrated with excellent drawings and diagrams of the tunnel complex and the construction equipment.

Official Eurotunnel Website
http://www.eurotunnel.co.uk
This website of Eurotunnel, the company that constructed the Channel Tunnel, contains information on schedules and booking passage. It also has a history of the company and a galley of photos of the tunnel's construction.

Spangenburg, Ray. *The Story of America's Tunnels*. New York: Replica Books, 1999.
Find out more about tunnels in the United States. This book details the history of tunnel building in the U.S., from the early Schuylkill Navigation Tunnel through the complex immersed-tube tunnels being built today.

Index

Sandy Donovan has written many books for young readers on topics including history, civics, and biology. She has worked as a newspaper reporter, a magazine editor, a labor market analyst, and an evaluation consultant. She has lived and traveled in Europe, Asia, and the Middle East and holds a bachelor's degree in journalism and a master's degree in public policy. She lives in Minneapolis, Minnesota, with her husband and son.

Photo Acknowledgments

The images in this book are used with the permission of: © Jim Byrne/ QAPHOTOS, pp. 1, 2–3, 4–5, 6, 7, 8 (inset), 24, 29, 32, 33, 34 (left), 37, 38, 41, 42–43, 45, 46, 48; © Stapleton Collection/CORBIS, pp. 8–9; Independent Picture Service, pp. 10–11; Library of Congress, p. 14; Laura Westlund, pp. 12, 22–23, 28–29, 33 (bottom); Hulton | Archive by Getty Images, pp. 15, 18 (inset); © Hulton-Deutsch Collection/CORBIS, p. 17; © Dean Conger/CORBIS, pp. 18–19; © Reuters NewMedia Inc./CORBIS, pp. 26–27; © Diana Craigie/QAPHOTOS, pp. 31; © Polak Matthew/CORBIS SYGMA, pp. 34–35; © Robby Whitfield/ QAPHOTOS, pp. 40, 42, 50–51; © Colin Garat; Milepost 92 ½/CORBIS, p. 48; © Nogues Alain/CORBIS SYGMA, p. 52; © CORBIS SYGMA, pp. 53, 59; © Trip/H. Rogers, pp. 54, 55, 56, 64, 65; AP/Wide World Photos; pp. 58, 62; © Trip/B. Turner, pp. 60–61.

Cover: © Jim Byrne/QAPHOTOS, diagram by Laura Westlund

Back cover: © Jim Byrne/QAPHOTOS